BOOK ANALYSIS

Written by Maël Tailler and Larissa Duval
Translated by Ciaran Traynor

AF 131383

Animal Farm
BY GEORGE ORWELL

GEORGE ORWELL

ENGLISH WRITER

- **Born in Motihari (British India) in 1903.**
- **Died in London in 1950.**
- **Notable works**:
  - *Homage to Catalonia* (1938), non-fiction
  - *Animal Farm* (1945), novel
  - *1984* (1949), novel

George Orwell (real name Eric Arthur Blair) was an English writer born in Motihari (British India) in 1903. After studying in England, he returned to India and joined the Imperial Police in Burma. He resigned in 1928 and decided to become a writer. He then spent several years drifting from Paris to London, where he lived alongside some of the poorest members of society (*Down and Out in Paris and London*, 1933). After this, he had several different jobs (bookseller, teacher, columnist) before signing up for the Spanish Civil War against fascism (*Homage to Catalonia*, 1938).

During the Second World War, he dedicated himself to journalism and wrote some of his most famous novels, including *Animal Farm* (1945) and *1984* (1949). Orwell died from tuberculosis in London in 1950.

ANIMAL FARM

A CRITIQUE OF POLITICAL POWER

- **Genre**: allegorical novel
- **Reference edition**: Orwell, G. (1993) *Animal Farm*. London: Everyman.
- **1st edition**: 1945
- **Themes**: utopia, communism, totalitarianism, equality, power

Animal Farm, published in 1945, is an allegorical novel which tells the story of a group of farm animals who overthrow their masters and ban all humans from their new land.

The text is actually a criticism of Stalinism and, more broadly, of totalitarianism, through the characters of the pigs who flout the egalitarian principles put in place during the revolt against the humans, and gradually install a system of oppression and exploitation which the other animals suffer from.

The novel is now extremely famous and is regarded as one of the classics of English literature.

SUMMARY

REVOLUTION

Once Mr Jones, the owner of Manor Farm, has gone to bed, the farm animals gather in the barn to listen to old Major, the pigs' elder, as it is the pigs who claim to be the most intelligent of all the animals. He invites his brethren to revolt against the only animal who consumes without producing and exploits all the others: man. The pig-prophet has even made a doctrine out of his ideas: Animalism. He had a dream which reminded him of an old song which heralds the golden age of animals: *Beasts of England*. He begins to sing it, and all the other animals join in enthusiastically, until Mr Jones, woken up by the din, fires a gunshot to scare off a potential fox. After old Major dies , Napoleon, Snowball and Squealer, three pigs who have taught themselves to read, set about teaching the other animals the alphabet and Animalism in order to lay the groundwork for the revolution.

This initiative does not take long to bear fruit: when Mr Jones neglects to feed the animals, they chase him off the farm along with his wife and workers. Now masters of the farm, they rush to get rid of all the instruments of oppression which have caused them so much suffering over the years and decide to run the place, now renamed "Animal Farm", themselves. The next day, before going to collect hay in the fields, the pigs write the Seven Commandments of Animalism on one of the walls:

- Whatever goes upon two legs is an enemy.

- Whatever goes upon four legs, or has wings, is a friend.
- No animal shall wear clothes.
- No animal shall sleep in a bed.
- No animal shall drink alcohol.
- No animal shall kill any other animal.
- All animals are equal.

On Sundays, the pigs preside over the Meeting and organise the life of the others. As most of the other animals cannot read, Snowball shortens the Seven Commandments to one: "Four legs good, two legs bad", which the sheep begin to chant non-stop. As for Napoleon, he stays in the background, but quietly rounds up and imprisons nine puppies who will be of great use to him during the coup he has been preparing in secret. Time passes and the pigs begin giving themselves more and more rights, claiming that, without them, it would be impossible to run the farm.

The other farmers in the vicinity quickly learn of the uprising from Mr Jones and begin to slander the animals, because the revolutionary song *Beasts of England* is making its way through the countryside. Mr Jones tries to take back his farm on 12 October with the help of a few henchmen. However, under Snowball's leadership, the animals manage to rout them and, from this day onwards, 12 October becomes a day of remembrance: The Day of the Battle of the Cowshed. Meanwhile, a lazy, pretty mare called Mollie leaves the farm for good after being accused of letting a human pet her.

TAKING POWER

January arrives and, during such a difficult season for all the animals, the rivalry between Snowball and Napoleon continues to grow. Snowball wants to build a mill and put greater emphasis on propaganda, while Napoleon sees this as a waste of time and insists on the importance of organising the defence of the farm. During one Meeting, Napoleon stages a coup thanks to the nine hounds that he brought up in secret, forcing Snowball into exile and causing the dissolution of the Meeting. From now on there is only a committee of pigs led by Napoleon who run the farm. Squealer, who is now Napoleon's spokesman, begins to rewrite history: according to him, Napoleon had always wanted to build a mill. Moving into Mr Jones' old house, the pigs revise and then begin to ignore the Seven Commandments, giving themselves new benefits while Squealer continues to wipe the animals' memories.

One year later, the animals are still working hard in the fields and on the construction of the mill. When they begin to run out of certain things from the outside world, Napoleon announces that he wants to do business with the neighbouring farms. In the outside world, the other farmers are amazed by the stability of Animal Farm, which they had at first made fun of.

One night in November, the mill is destroyed by a violent storm. Claiming that this is Snowball's doing, Napoleon sentences him to death. A rumour begins to spread that the exiled pig is back on the farm. When he finds out, Napoleon blames Snowball for all the farm's problems and Squealer makes him public enemy number one. The animals set about building a more solid mill, but when food begins to become scarce their enthusiasm wanes with it. In order to crush any potential revolt, Napoleon turns to his hounds to help him publicly execute several animals accused of being traitors. Moreover, *Beasts of England* is now banned because, according to Squealer, the revolution has succeeded. Realising that they have strayed too far from their initial goal, Clover, the mare, Benjamin, the sceptical donkey, and several others all give up on the revolution.

Work therefore goes on, but only Napoleon, the pigs and the dogs benefit from it. In autumn, the mill is completed. However, contrary to general belief, it will not be used to improve life on the farm. Napoleon has made a deal to sell wood to a neighbouring farmer called Frederick. But Frederick betrays him and, the next day, attacks the farm with even more men and guns than Mr Jones had brought. And so begins the Battle of the Windmill. The animals emerge victorious, but suffer heavy losses: in addition to the deaths and casualties, the mill is also destroyed. Over the next few days, the pigs celebrate their victory with parties and get drunk on whisky. Squealer continues to alter the Seven Commandments: "No animal shall drink alcohol" is now amended with the words "to excess."

ANIMALS? OR MEN?

That year's winter is harsher than the previous one and rations continue to decrease. Napoleon develops his cult of personality and organises ceremonies. He proclaims a Republic and makes himself President. Meanwhile, certain animals begin to think about their retirement. One of the horses, the well-meaning but rather dim Boxer, was injured during the battle and has to be taken to a vet. However, it is not a vet who comes to collect him, but a butcher. Benjamin tries to stop the truck, in vain. In order to put the animals' consciences at rest, Squealer once again alters the story, and Napoleon organises a banquet in honour of their fallen brother.

The years go by, and there are now few animals remaining who still remember the days before the uprising. Many are dead; none have retired. The mill has finally been finished, and the farm is now more prosperous. However, the profits are enjoyed only by the dogs and the pigs. One day, while the sheep are chanting another slogan, "Four legs good, two legs better", Napoleon and the other pigs come out from the house on two legs. Benjamin then reads Clover the only Commandment left on the wall of the cowshed: "All animals are equal, but some animals are more equal than others". Bit by bit, the pigs begin to use the clothes and tools left behind by the men, including whips. One night, during a banquet with the neighbouring farmers, Napoleon declares that he has modified the symbol and the name of the farm. It is now once again called Manor Farm. Watching the scene from the window, Clover and some of the others realise that they can no longer tell the pigs from the men.

CHARACTER STUDY

Animal Farm can be read as a roman à clef: it is an allegorical representation of the history of the Soviet Union in the first half of the 20th century. Here, we will highlight certain parallels between fictional characters of the novel and important figures from history (although this is by no means an exhaustive list).

THE SOVIET UNION

In 1917, tired of poverty under the rule of Tsar Nicholas II (due to World War I, backwardness, poverty and famine), the Russian people rebelled and set up the world's first Communist regime. Communism is a political doctrine created by the revolutionary socialist Karl Marx (1818-1883).

It is a model of society founded on the abolition'of social classes and private property, where wealth and status are shared equally among everyone. On the economic side of things, instead of responding to supply and demand, production (agriculture, industrial, and so on) is planned and controlled by the State, which has a stranglehold on practically everything that goes on in the country.

Although it began with noble intentions, Russian Communism quickly turned into a totalitarian regime. After around ten years of more or less successful reforms (mainly in agriculture and industry), Stalin took power for himself and reigned over the country as its only leader. He ousted all opponents (real and imagined) through show trials, and established revolutionary propaganda, the manipulation of information and history, the cult of personality, gulags (work camps), and so on.

After World War II, the USSR took advantage of the German defeat to set up Communist (and dictatorial) regimes across Eastern Europe. Despite Stalin's death in 1953, these regimes stayed in place until 1989, the year of the fall of the Berlin Wall. Today, Cuba, China and North Korea are the last countries to still have Communist regimes, which are however a long way from the original Marxist doctrine.

THE MEN

Mr Jones

The owner and manager of Manor Farm, Mr Jones often exploits his animals. However, he begins to lose his motivation to work, turning to alcohol and forgetting to feed the livestock. The animals then revolt and force him into exile. He could be a representation of Tsar Nicholas II: neglecting his people and incapable of reforming the Russian Empire. The Tsar was eventually faced with the February Revolution in 1917 and was forced to abdicate.

The neighbouring farmers: Frederick and Pilkington

Frederick, the owner of Pinchfield farm, has a German-sounding name. He realises that the time for slander has passed and secretly makes a deal with the pigs (on the selling of wood) before betraying them and trying to invade their farm. Frederick therefore calls to mind Hitler, who, in spite of the Nazi–Soviet Pact (an agreement for non-aggression between Hitler and Stalin signed in 1939), attempted to conquer the Soviet Union.

Pilkington, the owner of Foxwood Farm, is described as a "gentleman farmer". Although he does not trust Animal Farm, he also tries to discreetly make a deal with them. Pilkington could be a representation of Churchill, seeing as he is at the head of "a large, neglected, old-fashioned farm" rather reminiscent of the British Empire.

Although Frederick and Pilkington are both opposed to Animalism, they are still incapable of co-operating with one another, just like the men they represent.

THE PIGS

Old Major

Old Major is the most enlightened and venerated of all the animals. At the start of the story, he envisions a more just society free of man (the exploiter), where the animals (who he calls "comrades") are all equal, govern themselves and share what they have among one another. An allegorical reading of the text indicates that old Major represents Marx, whose philosophy has greatly influenced modern

Marxism (particularly the idea of the proletariat – the animals –overthrowing the ruling class – men).

Napoleon

Napoleon is a determined, "large, rather fierce-looking Berkshire boar", and not much of a talker. He is an authoritative pig who quickly overthrows the egalitarian regime put in place after the rebellion and replaces it with a dictatorship with the help of his army of dogs. In many respects (his cult of personality, reign of terror, political purges, rewriting history, and so on), this "Father of all Animals" bears a resemblance to the "Little father of the peoples": Stalin.

Snowball

Snowball is a "vivacious" pig. Preferring words over weapons, he tries to educate the animals and organise the farm. He sincerely wants to improve his friends' living conditions (with the mill, for example) and fights courageously during the Battle of the Cowshed. Taking into account his exile, his death sentence, the defamation campaign organised against him and his will to spread the revolution to other farms, he seems more like Trotsky than Lenin.

Squealer

Squealer, a "small, fat pig", stands out from the other pigs due to his talkativeness (he is called Squealer, after all) and his powers of persuasion. A venal little pig, it does not take him long to join the strongest side – Napoleon's, who he quickly becomes the spokesperson of. He is the embodiment of the organs of Soviet propaganda (like the daily newspaper *Pravda*), which were tasked with rewriting history and promoting the regime.

THE DOGS

The nine hounds raised by Napoleon and then given preferential treatment on the farm make up the forces of order. They represent Stalin's political police.

THE SHEEP

The sheep are incapable of thinking for themselves and constantly chant the slogans they are given, without realising that they are often contradictory or against their own interests. Take the initial "Four legs good, two legs bad", for example, which eventually morphs into "four legs good, two legs better", without them so much as batting an eyelid. The sheep (which are generally seen as conformist animals) represent the indoctrinated masses.

BOXER THE HORSE

As his name implies, Boxer stands out due to his strength. Courageous, if a little dim and naïve, the cart-horse gives it his all in the fields and during the (re)construction of the mill. His mottos are "I will work harder!" (he sleeps less in order to get work done faster) and "Napoleon is always right" (he is incapable of imagining his leader trying to manipulate him). Boxer represents the productive, militant workers who were devoted to the regime and yet were still exploited (in the USSR, Stakhanovism, from the name of a particularly productive miner who was glorified by the Stalinist regime, was used to describe this doctrine of putting work above everything else).

MOSES THE RAVEN

Tamed by Mr Jones, Moses the raven tells anyone who will listen that there is a place in the next life called Sugarcandy Mountain, a better world where everyone goes after death. He is there when the animals need to believe in something to keep going: at the start of the tale, when they are starving because of the farmer's laziness; and, at the end, when they are miserable again, oppressed by the pigs. Although he is looked down on by the pigs, they use him and his stories to keep the animals under their yoke, promising them that if they work hard without complaining, they will be allowed to go to this incredible place in this next life.

A character bringing comfort to the oppressed while also serving the interests of those in power, Moses the raven represents the clergy of the Russian Orthodox Church.

ANALYSIS

An apologue is a short allegorical tale with an argumentative or didactic aim and a moral. While *Animal Farm* is a novel first and foremost, it also has most of the characteristics of an apologue.

Simplicity

An apologue is a short tale with an easy-to-understand plot, simple language and a small number of characters, who are often stereotyped (animals, for example, in the sub-genre of the fable).

Animal Farm follows many of the rules of an apologue:

- it is indeed a short tale (ten chapters and a total of 116 pages) and is written in language that everyone can understand;
- the story can be summed up in a few words (animals take control of a farm, where they create an equal society before a group of pigs bring back dictatorship);
- The characters are animals which represent the different social classes (the pigs are the lazy leaders, the sheep embody the stupid, conformist and submissive people, the cart-horses are hard-working and docile, and so on).

A book with two meanings

An apologue takes the form of a long extended metaphor, since the characters and the situations have more meaning than they first appear to have.

Animal Farm represents human society, particularly a specific human society at a precise moment in history: Russia (and then the USSR) in the first half of the 20th century. Moreover, the characters are all based on real people. For example, Napoleon is a dominant pig who embodies the figure of the dictator, a character similar to Stalin in a number of ways.

The argumentative dimension

The narrative outline of an apologue is set up in such a way as to highlight an idea.

Animal Farm has a clear message: the rebellion has failed and the pigs have taken advantage of the situation to slowly establish a regime that is just as bad as, or even worse than, that of Mr Jones. This idea is presented to the reader in different ways:

- The clear opposition between the good (the horses, the donkey, the chickens) and bad (the dogs, the pigs – with the exception of old Major and Snowball – and, to a certain extent, the sheep) characters.
- The sense of escalation as the chapters go by, with the injustices and acts of violence against the oppressed (by Napoleon and his dogs), the disregard for the law as set out in old Major's speech, the transformation of the story

of the Battle of the Cowshed (by Squealer), the growing inequalities, and the pigs' imitation of men.
- The omniscient, faux-objective narrator (he discreetly points out Squealer's cynicism, for example).
- The cyclical structure of the book. Chapter 10 clearly links back to Chapter 1. The narrator assesses the situation compared with the days before the uprising and shows that little has changed: the animals are still exploited and miserable; the pigs behave like men; the farm has returned to its original name; inequality is once again the name of the game.

Teaching or reflection

An apologue aims to educate readers with a certain moral (explicit or implicit) or a certain truth (about men, society or even the world).

Although *Animal Farm* does have an educational side to it (the reader is shown that a generous utopia can be distorted and insidiously replaced with a brutal totalitarian regime), its moral is rather implicit, or even absent at times. Indeed, there is no attitude or act which can improve the situation: not optimism (Boxer, Clover), nor pessimism (Benjamin), nor escape (Mollie, Snowball), nor submission (the majority), nor timid revolt (the executed 'traitors'). Fatalism is all that is left: equality between the animals is an illusion, since some will always be "more equal than others."

The different forms of an apologue

An apologue can take different forms: fable, fabliau, parable, utopia, tale or short story. Although *Animal Farm* is a novel, and therefore not one of the genres on this list, it can simply be considered a new form of apologue.

A DENUNCIATION OF TOTALITARIANISM

From parallels with Soviet history...

Animal Farm draws parallels with many major events in Russian history.

Chapter of the book	Part of the novel	Parallel in the history of the USSR
1	The animals are exploited by Mr Jones; old Major shares his dream	Tsarism (Nicholas II); spread of the revolutionary ideas of Marx
2-3	The animals rebel and organise their new Animal Farm; the song *Beasts of England* is sung at the end of every Meeting	February and October Revolutions of 1917, and establishment of the Soviet Union; the *Internationale*, the revolutionary song of the working classes, becomes the national anthem of the USSR
4	Battle of the Cowshed (during which Mr Jones is backed by Frederick and Pilkington's men)	War against the White Armies (made up of tsarists, monarchists and republicans backed by foreign forces)
5	Rivalry between Snowball and Napoleon; Snowball is forced to flee	Rivalry between Trotsky and Stalin; Trotsky is persecuted and goes into exile
6-7	Napoleon's reign of terror begins; execution of traitors; directives from the Sunday Meeting and construction of the mill	Stalinism; Moscow Trials; five-year-plans and modernisation of the USSR

Animal Farm © BrightSummaries.com

Chapter of the book	Part of the novel	Parallel in the history of the USSR
8	Napoleon is not sure whether he should make a deal with Frederick or Pilkington (on the selling of wood), then Frederick tries to invade Animal Farm, but fails	During the Second World War, Stalin was not sure whether to ally himself with England or Germany; the Nazis invaded the USSR, but were pushed back
9-10	Napoleon continues his reign of terror, the farm becomes more prosperous and also even more unequal. Finally, the men are invited to eat with the pigs	After the war, Stalinism becomes tougher and the USSR expands to other countries. Stalin and the elite continue to get richer while diplomacy is once again established with other countries (The Yalta Conference, February 1945)

... to an overall analysis of the mechanisms of power

However, the novel is not merely a carbon copy of Russian history. Several conflicting elements suggest that this is not the only reading we can make of the book (the dictator is called Napoleon, the story takes place in the English countryside, the revolt took place in June while the Russian Revolutions happened in February and October 1917, and so on).

In *Animal Farm*, the author conveys his scepticism and pessimism not only in regard to socialism, which he had strongly supported in his youth (in fact, Orwell was one of the first European intellectuals to denounce Stalinism at a time when European democracies were trying to avoid offending the dictator at all costs and refused to see the vices of the regime), but more generally regarding political power. As we are told, "politics [by] their nature are inseparable from coercion and fraud" (Angus and Orwell, 1970: 463). This is essential to our understanding of the eventual resemblance of the pigs to the men: in the end, ideology matters little, as long as you have power. And power goes hand in hand with inequality, corruption and the betrayal of the initial ideals.

Behind a seemingly innocent premise (an apologue with talking farm animals), Orwell exposes, in an almost didactic way, how a generous utopia can bring about the worst of political regimes.

LANGUAGE AS A MEANS OF OPPRESSION

With *Animal Farm*, Orwell therefore studies the different mechanisms which allow a minority to turn revolution to its own advantage. One of the ways the pigs strengthen their hold on the others is using language to manipulate them.

The use of language to rally the others to a specific cause can be seen from the outset, with old Major's speech, which uses different rhetorical techniques to convince his audience:

- he begins by introducing himself as someone wise,

someone whose opinion matters, and at the same time puts himself on an equal footing with the others by calling them his "comrades";

- he moves on to describe the animals' miserable situation with a great deal of insistence;
- he plays on their feelings by pointing out that things do not have to stay the way they are: they can be better;
- he blames all their problems on one single enemy: Man;
- he simplifies his speech as far as possible, setting out only one objective ("Only get rid of Man, and the produce of our labour would be our own") and a short series of slogans – which become the Seven Commandments;
- he creates a sense of community through song with *Beasts of England*.

In this case, however, rhetoric is used with the aim of sharing a noble ideal, without any ulterior motives.

Afterwards, the pigs turn the foundations old Major has laid to their advantage and manipulate information. Through the use of propaganda, the leaders are able to make the population believe that the situation cannot be changed: it is as it is and cannot be better. The animals should therefore be happy with their lot and be grateful to the pigs. Squealer is the one who embodies this propaganda most of all, and he does not hesitate to use several techniques in his manipulation of the animals' hearts and minds:

- The use of fear makes the animals go along with some of their dictates (they play on the fear of Mr Jones' return, for example).
- The spreading of false figures makes the animals believe

that they are better fed than before.

- The extreme simplification of the principles to remember, like the Seven Commandments, which are themselves eventually shortened to the slogan "four legs good, two legs bad".
- The use of convoluted explanations, with words which are too complex for the animals to understand, allow the pigs to sow confusion and make even the most absurd line of reasoning appear logical. As a result, it seems clear that the pigs are only giving themselves certain luxuries for the common good. "When it was put to them in this light, they [the animals] had no more to say".
- The gradual rewriting of the Seven Commandments and the maxim (which becomes "four legs good, two legs better") is used in the interests of the dominant group.
- The attribution of different honorific titles to Napoleon, as well as the composition of poems and speeches lauding his personality, is supposed to create a real cult of personality centred around him.

Obviously, there is a clear criticism of the USSR, which very often manipulated information (with censorship, the fabrication of evidence in Stalin's show trials, false propaganda, and so on). Moreover, one of the keys to this process is the falsification of history (revisionism): many communists who had fallen into disgrace with Stalin were killed and literally erased from collective memory (photos they were in were altered to remove them, for example). In the same way, the pigs do not think twice about rewriting the Seven Commandments, even though they were supposed to be unchangeable.

Orwell's call to be vigilant against propaganda's ability to get into people's minds, even the minds of the educated, is not limited to the USSR. The kind of demagogic indoctrination Squealer uses, with his meaningless – though rousing – speeches, is not limited to dictatorial regimes: the neighbouring farms (which mostly symbolise capitalist democracies) do the same thing. Orwell is warning us against all the often insidious ways information can be manipulated so as to dodge the real questions and establish a certain reality as if it were the one, unchangeable truth.

FURTHER REFLECTION

SOME QUESTIONS TO THINK ABOUT...

- In what way can *Animal Farm* be viewed as an apologue?
- What does the story symbolise? Develop the main elements which allow us to determine this.
- The animals on the farm act differently according to their species. What type of person or reaction can each of them be associated with?
- Orwell presents us with an extremely pertinent analysis of Communism. In what way is this analysis still valid in the decades which followed the novel's release?
- Is Communism the only thing that Orwell is trying to denounce? Base your answer on the biographical elements and the author's other books.
- How can language be described as one of the key elements of the novel?
- Which important figures from history are alluded to in the novel?
- Is the novel's denunciation of Communism still relevant today? Justify and develop your answer.
- Compare *Animal Farm* to Voltaire's *Candide*. How can we see the influence of the Enlightenment in the novel?
- Compare *Animal Farm* to Pink Floyd's album *Animals*. Which elements allow us to say that the album is a reference to Orwell's novel? Explain how the group managed to make reference to *Animal Farm*.

We want to hear from you!
Leave a comment on your online library
and share your favourite books on social media!

FURTHER READING

REFERENCE EDITION

- Orwell, G. (1993) *Animal Farm*. London: Everyman.

REFERENCE STUDY

- Angus, I. and Orwell, S. (1970) *The Collected Essays, Journalism and Letters of George Orwell, vol. IV*. London: Secker & Warburg.

ADAPTATIONS

- *Animal Farm*. (1954) [film]. Halas and Batchelor, dir. United Kingdom: Halas and Batchelor.
- *Animals*. (1977) [sound recording]. Performed by Pink Floyd. London: Harvest, Columbia.
- Various theatre adaptations, notably in Paris and London.

MORE FROM BRIGHTSUMMARIES.COM

- Reading guide – *1984* by George Orwell.

www.brightsummaries.com

Ebook EAN: 9782806294913

Paperback EAN: 9782806294920

Legal Deposit: D/2017/12603/136

This guide was written with the collaboration of Larissa Duval for the chapters 'Moses the raven' '... to an overall analysis of the mechanics of power' and 'Language as a means of oppression'.

Cover: © Primento

Digital conception by Primento, the digital partner of publishers.